CHILDE HAROLD
OF DYSNA

CHILDE HAROLD
OF **DYSNA**

Moyshe Kulbak

TRANSLATED FROM THE YIDDISH BY
Robert Adler Peckerar

WITH AN INTRODUCTION BY
Boris Dralyuk

ILLUSTRATIONS BY
Beynish

Naydus Press
Cincinnati, Ohio
2020

Published 2020 by Naydus Press
Printed in the United States of America
Cover design by Sarah Miner
Cover illustration courtesy of the Stadtgeschichtliches Museum Leipzig,
Germany (*1. Mai 1929; Postkarte | Leipziger Buchdruckerei AG (Verlag) |
Stadtgeschichtliches Museum Leipzig, Germany | CC-BY-NC-SA*)

First Edition

Naydus Press is a non-profit, 501(c)(3) organization dedicated to
increasing awareness of and access to Yiddish literature by supporting
Yiddish translators and publishing their translations into English.
Our goal is to bring the best of Yiddish literature to new generations
of readers.

ISBN 978-1-7341936-0-2

FOR

Eli Katz

CONTENTS

ACKNOWLEDGEMENTS

Naydus Press wishes to express its gratitude to these donors for their financial support:

Robert and Caryl Gorman
John E. Sands
Delphine Katz
The Annenberg Foundation

INTRODUCTION

Pipe Dreams: On Moyshe Kulbak's *Childe Harold of Dysna*

If poetry, as Wordsworth wrote, is at its root "emotion recollected in tranquillity," then Moyshe Kulbak's *Childe Harold of Dysna* (1928–1933) stands as a marvelous—if rather skewed and distinctly twentieth-century—exemplar of the genre. How else could one describe this boisterous mock-epic of a Belarusian boychik's formative misadventures in Weimar Berlin, recollected, at a decade's remove, by a respected teacher and man of letters in Soviet Minsk? But of course this poem is nothing like what Wordsworth had in mind . . . As Kulbak's title suggests, a different sort of Romanticism hovers over these sixty-two sonnet-like cantos—the ironic Romanticism of Lord Byron.

Yes, there is indeed a Byronic streak to our hero, "our noble Pipeman," who sets out on the train from Dysna (or is it Lohojsk? or Narovlya? or Smorgon?) with nothing but a "shirt, some smokes, high-flying poems" and, midway through his German sojourn, manages to net a "blonde, young bird from Tauenzienstraße," who mistakes him for "the Cossack, Herr Kriuchkov." Pipeman ticks off a lot of Byronic boxes—his "longing is fashionable," he "gazes with dark and tender eyes"—yet something's off, not quite kosher. Perhaps *too* kosher.

There's more dopey pretense to Pipeman than brooding

heroism. He's prone to Walter Mitty–like flights of fancy: "While wandering his hometown aimless [. . .] He tailed all like Pinkerton the shamus." But what else do you expect of a fellow who's been "Absorbed in novels and poetic diction / For nineteen years"? Here I sense Kulbak's debt not only to Byron, the trailblazer of Byronism, but to his wittiest inheritor, the great Russian poet Alexander Pushkin, whose Eugene Onegin was weaned on the Englishman's verse. In his attempt to act out Byronic ideals on Russian soil, Onegin shatters his only real chance at happiness. The fate that awaits young Pipeman in Berlin is not so personally tragic, but this too is a tale of inapplicable literary models—a subject to which I will return. But let's not leave Pipeman hanging. Who is he?

To answer that question, permit me to descend from the sublime to the ridiculous—or from the ridiculous to the still more ridiculous. As I read Robert Adler Peckerar's pyrotechnic translation of Kulbak's verse tale, which radiates with irrepressible ebullience and hints at deep wells of melancholy, I thought of a line from Wes Anderson's film *Rushmore* (1998). When the ambitious schoolboy, Max Fischer, falls from the great heights of Rushmore Academy and, briefly, resigns himself to the social position from which he had clambered up so tenaciously, he rejects his working-class father's encouragement with a staccato lament worthy of Clifford Odets: "Pipe dreams, Dad. I'm a barber's son."

Our hero's origins—and, at times, his attitude—are not dissimilar: "There wafts from him a tailor's scent / Bequeathed by legacies of toil and want." Our hero knows it. And as much as he would sometimes like to forget it, in the end he always embraces it—as he does in this sweet, brilliant monologue to his Fräulein, disabusing her of the notion that he is the steely Herr Kriuchkov:

> I'm just a Cossack who's come from Shklov;
> *Mein Papa war ein alter Kavalier*
> *Von Iron-Shears*, known for slinging
> Taters out of white-hot flames,

And, as is the Order of Needles' fame,
He accompanied life with song and singing . . .

Just as he can't shake his origins, so too does he remain an inveterate bookworm. One senses that, despite all the hubbub around him, most of his time is spent "Palely shiver[ing] on the sofa, / Surrounded by books and newspapers." And if he and his buddies wind up in the clink, it's "After having made a scene" by "Pars[ing] Hegesias of Cyrene" in a drunken state. This is not to say that Pipeman is dull to the stimuli of Weimar life. The commercial and intellectual frenzy of postwar Berlin, which Kulbak describes so vividly, makes his head spin:

O Wond'rous Land! Where electricity passes
Through wires, and through arteries—champagne—
Where Marx and Engels cheer the working masses
And shop-keeps swear by Kant's immortal name.

It all makes him "feel just like an air-balloon, / Whose string is loosened, and set free." So who is our wide- and dewy-eyed Pipeman, with his bookish fantasies? Childe Harold? Don Juan? Mazeppa? More like an overeducated Menachem-Mendl. A uniquely Kulbakian luftmensch.

·:·

Unlike his not quite placeable alter ego, Moyshe Kulbak was born in a certain town, at a certain time: on March 20, 1896, in Smorgon (now Smarhon', Belarus), which was then part of the Russian Empire. The town's cultural roots were Lithuanian and Polish, but by the time of Kulbak's birth, some three quarters of its 7,500 inhabitants were Jewish. Kulbak received a solid education in a Russian state-run Jewish school, attending a *cheder* in the evenings, and also studied, briefly, at the famed Volozhin yeshiva—but he was forced to return home after the outbreak of the First World War, and then relocated to Kovno (now Kaunas,

Lithuania), where he taught Hebrew in the Jewish school for orphans.

Kulbak's literary passions were at first fueled by the Hebrew-revivalist ideas of Ahad Ha'am, and he continued to work on his Hebrew in Kovno, but he soon switched to Yiddish. It was in Yiddish that he made his debut in 1916, with the poem "Little Star" ("*Shterndl*"), a Jewish soldier's prayer and lament from the front. By the time he reached Vilna (now Vilnius, Lithuania) in 1919, he was already considered a bright literary light, and he cemented that reputation in 1920, with the publication of *Verses* (*Shirim*).

That same year Kulbak hied himself and his "high-flying poems" to Berlin. As Rachel Seelig reports in her fine study *Strangers in Berlin: Modern Jewish Literature Between East and West, 1919–1933*, Kulbak aimed "to immerse himself in Berlin's thriving cultural life." When he announced, in a letter to the literary critic Shmuel Niger, that he had arrived in "EUROPE" writ large, he "was speaking not only for himself but also for Yiddish poetry [. . .]. Implicit in his individual artistic aspirations was the broader cultural mission of enriching a relatively undeveloped Yiddish poetic tradition." Alas, as Seelig puts it, "Kulbak's enthusiastic arrival did not correspond to his overall experience of Berlin."[1]

During his three years in Weimar Germany, Kulbak's imagination, like that of many artists in exile, drew him homeward. His work from the period is suffused with a mystical, lyrical devotion to nature—namely, to the natural landscape of his Belarusian Jewish childhood and youth. And yet, as Jordan Finkin writes in his sensitive, penetrating essay on Kulbak's "Berlin poetics," the city certainly impacted the texture of the young poet's largely nostalgic verse: "The heterogeneity of the forms and genres [of *New Poems* (*Naye lider*, 1922)] reflects Kulbak's experimentation with providing Yiddish with a poetic diversity

1. Rachel Seelig, *Strangers in Berlin: Modern Jewish Literature Between East and West, 1919–1933* (Ann Arbor: University of Michigan Press, 2016), p. 79.

equal to the European literatures with which he was in increasing contact in the metropolis."[2]

The seed had been planted. The new modes of European poetry—and especially of German Expressionism—that Kulbak had encountered in Berlin would continue to germinate in his work long after he returned to Vilna in 1923, destitute and depressed. And they would come to full flower in the most unexpected of places, Soviet Minsk, to which he and his young family would immigrate in 1928.

It was in Minsk that Kulbak once again looked backward—this time not to his Belarusian childhood, but to his wild days in Berlin. And it is Minsk that accounts for that key element of *Childe Harold* that I have not yet addressed: the tension between its exuberant Expressionistic imagery and ribald, ironic Byronism on the one hand, and its heartbreakingly heartfelt leftism on the other. For Kulbak's poem is as rich in its rage at police brutality and disgust at bourgeois hypocrisy as it is lavish in its style:

> France has steel that's stainless,
> Belgium coke and Germany lead.
> So often the worker wracked by pain is
> Led to the abattoir, left for dead.
> The old prisons have devoured us,
> Just like you, O Fatherland Great,
> Neukölln sings its hate. [. . .]

The last sound we hear is that of the radicals, "the last of wolves that bay / In the ruins of the system."

All this seems right for a poem written in Minsk between the years 1928 and 1933—but once again, something's off. "Thematically," writes Seelig, "it accords with the Soviet party

---

2. Jordan Finkin, "'Like Fires in Overgrown Forests': Moyshe Kulbak's Contemporary Berlin Poetics," in *Yiddish in Weimar Berlin: At the Crossroads of Diaspora Politics and Culture*, ed. by Gennady Estraikh and Mikhail Krutikov (London: Legenda, 2010), pp. 73–88.

line. Yet the use of avant-garde literary techniques distinguishes this work from the propagandistic 'proletarian' Soviet Yiddish literature gaining prominence in Minsk and throughout the Soviet Union."[3]

This tension distinguishes the poem, yes—but it also puts it in conversation with other exhilaratingly ambiguous master-pieces of the era, such as Isaac Babel's *Red Cavalry* (1926), David Bergelson's novel *Judgment* (1929), and Kulbak's own *The Zelmenyaners: A Family Saga* (1931), all of which are available in English. Eighty-two years after Kulbak's death in Stalin's purges, Adler Peckerar has done readers of English a great service by adding the poet's immortal *Childe Harold of Dysna* to that illustrious colloquy.

Boris Dralyuk
Los Angeles
AUGUST 2019

---

3. Seelig, p. 98.

TRANSLATOR'S FOREWORD

The *Childe Harold of Dysna* is the most ambitious poetic proj-
ect of the great Yiddish poet Moyshe Kulbak. It picks up the
various thematic strands from all of his previous poetic work,
especially those he had produced during, or which were inspired
by, his youthful adventure in Weimar Berlin in the early 1920s.
Together with his favorite poetic Belarusian and Jewish folk
motifs, Kulbak weaves in elements from Byron, Goethe, and
Heine, as well as his contemporary modernist German and
Russian poets. In the sixty-two twelve-line stanzas that follow,
Kulbak tells of a young provincial Jew's journey from a ruined
White Russian shtetl to metropolitan Berlin and of the descent
of a European literary capital—the Central European cultural
Parnassus, as it was known then—into the abyss of fascism
and violence.

This magnum opus marked a shift in Kulbak's poetry, sepa-
rating it from his earlier longer works, which were more often
modeled on traditional Eastern European long-form poemas. In
his *Childe Harold*, Kulbak's narrative unfolds through the consciousness of one character instead of through sweeping cinematic and kaleidoscopic overviews, typical of his earlier poetry.
This hero, whose naive eyes swallow up the glimmering cosmo-
politan life completely unknown to him, recognizes not only his

detachment from his new big-city life, but from himself as well. The protagonist of *Childe Harold* is a figure who hopes to find in Berlin the possibility of the new and the opportunity of radical self-invention in German culture. In the end, however, he finds only decadence.

Kulbak's Childe Harold is alternately called Shmulik Pipeman as well as "the Childe Harold" of several White Russian towns and villages, including Dysna, Lohojsk, Narovlya, and the poet's actual hometown of Smorgon. When Kulbak was composing the poem, most of these towns were in the recently-formed Byelorussian Soviet Socialist Republic, where Kulbak lived in its capital Minsk, but other towns, including the titular Dysna, were now found in the newly-constituted Polish Commonwealth. In refusing to assign any single geographical origin for the hero, Kulbak creates a Jewish White Russian Everyman. The poem is loosely modeled thematically and structurally, of course, after Byron's *Childe Harold's Pilgrimage* (1812–1818) but also on Heine's *Deutschland: ein Wintermärchen* (1844) and is divided into seven cantos. The first four are fully set in the consciousness of the hero, while the last three are overviews of the disintegration of German society and the failure of reason and humanism in the capital—all written in the decade that followed Kulbak's actual sojourn in Berlin from the autumn of 1920 until early in 1923. Although Pipeman is a composite of the young, politically progressive Jews with artistic aspirations who poured into Berlin, many details in the first two cantos correspond to Kulbak's life in the metropolis.

The flow of the poem is marked by an increasing discord between the young idealistic hero and the cynical narrator, making clear the distance of the poet in ideology and also time from his hero. Pipeman never fully becomes part of Berlin life, but rather remains a tourist watching from the sidelines of the café or from the roof of a double-decker bus. His appreciation of Germany is limited to images of classical Germanness represented by the figures of Goethe and Heine. Pipeman at first remains almost ignorant of the gap between the classically humanist and liberal culture that he came to study and the decadent reality of German cabaret life. Pipeman invites a comparison with the Christopher Isherwood figure who arrives in the Weimar Republic of *Goodbye to Berlin* ten years after Kulbak and famously declares: "I am a camera with its shutter open, quite passive, recording, not thinking."

In such a way, Pipeman seems to absorb images without expressly commenting on them, while the narrator's voice soundly derides the social reality that lies beneath. As with Isherwood, the wild cabaret scenes transform into grotesque and repulsive Otto Dix-style representations of the "masters of the marketplaces" and the sounds of a Black musician playing jazz, becoming representations of the violent German colonization of Africa.

The German colonial enterprise in Africa is referenced again in the lengthy "Goethe Day" section of the poem. When Pipeman's elderly landlady invites Pipeman to help mark Goethe's birthday by engaging with the great German poet, the everyday colloquial register of the poem shifts into an exaggeratedly highfalutin poetic diction, ironically thematizing Goethe's elevated status. This section marks a turning point in Pipeman's relation to German culture and becomes a meditation on the protagonist's disappointment in the contemporary conditions of German culture. Our young poet sees the ideals of Goethe's *Geist* in the fossilized reverence for the poet's work now as irrelevant as a poetic quote embroidered on a handkerchief in the pocket of jackbooted German soldiers.

The last cantos of the poem are set in the workers' districts—separated from the other cantos in their cinematic technique and observed from a distance rather than directly through the eyes of Childe Harold. In these last sections of the poem, it becomes clearer that these were composed at a distance in time and space from the Berlin that Kulbak knew ten years prior to writing the work. A long canto is devoted to an account of the *Blutmai* [Bloody May] rioting in the proletarian neighborhood of Wedding that took place on 1 May 1929, years after Kulbak had lived in the city, which left thirty-three people dead and hundreds injured. In this politically-driven violence, Kulbak retrospectively prophecies the imminence of fascist disaster.

Examining the seething districts of Berlin in these cantos, Kulbak sets the stage for the theme of the final sections of the poem, "The Other Germany." In presenting two Germanys, Kulbak introduces the notion of a historical shining, enlightened Germany that the Childe Harold set out to find, contrasting sharply with its opposite: the decaying bourgeois state brimming with the rage of the working masses. In such a presentation, Kulbak's initial laudatory view of the teeming and exciting city is recast retrospectively as a façade behind which hides a crumbling society. Here, Kulbak leans heavily on Heine's *Deutschland*.

In the twelfth chapter of Heine's poem, the speaker addresses a pack of wolves he comes across while traveling through the woods at night. Political readings of the poem have characterized the wolves as representative of "radical communists." Just as Heine proclaims, even ironically, to be a part of a pack of revolutionary wolves, so does the Childe Harold of Dysna declare himself part of a pack of wolves nearly a century after Heine. Instead of being confronted by these wildly howling beasts from a distance in the woods, Kulbak's speaker continues Heine's howling while stranded in the ruins of the destroyed idea of Germany. Howling with or in the spirit of Heine, Kulbak continues a poetic tradition of a radical voice whose hope is ultimately crushed.

Kulbak's *Childe Harold* is a meditation on loss. Our hero has experienced the loss of his hometown—both in the physical leaving of it, but also in its hinted destruction in the First World War. He has also taken leave of Berlin and lost hope in its exciting promise. In her most famous poem, "One Art," Elizabeth Bishop wrote: "I lost two cities, lovely ones. And, vaster, / some realms I owned, two rivers, a continent. / I miss them, but it wasn't a disaster." The Childe Harold, too, has lost two cities, one real and the other, perhaps, more imaginary, as well as entire landscapes decimated by the recent war and violence. Composed in the distance of time and space from the unfolding disillusionment he experienced, Kulbak's poem reflects a quiet despair in a world potentially headed towards even further ruin. Bishop's poem concludes: "It's evident / the art of losing's not too hard to master / though it may look like (*Write* it!) like disaster."

The conclusion of Kulbak's *Childe Harold* similarly writes a farewell to the allures of liberal humanism represented by the modern German metropolis and embraces a new revolutionary setting potentially possible only in the poet's chosen home in the Soviet Union. After the Nazi ascent to power in January 1933 when Kulbak sat down to compose his reflections of his time in the once-alluring Berlin, it was no longer possible to embrace what had attracted him there a decade earlier. The "system," according to Kulbak, lay in ruins already years before the ascent of the fascists. For Kulbak, there was no hope to be found in the rotting capitalist systems of the world, and Jewish culture could no longer benefit from the once-appealing German brand of liberality. The Soviet Union, especially in the cities filled with the Jews of White Russia, offered a potential new system that would attract writers and artists with its promise of liberation through creative expression in the Yiddish language. Four years later, Kulbak was declared an enemy of his beloved Soviet Union, arrested, and executed in the woods outside of Minsk.

Robert Adler Peckerar
AUTUMN 2019

CHILDE HAROLD
OF DYSNA

I.

A TRAIN

1.

A train. A window. A beaming glance.
A pipe clenched stiffly between two lips.
A young lad ventured out to find romance
With nothing but a set of ribs.
And in his pockets all he had:
A shirt, some smokes, high-flying poems.
Likewise embarked his tailor-dad,
With just his prayer-book, leaving home.
The wheels spin round—tum-tum-tum-tum.
And empires waver, powers are shifting!
It's grand, he thought. That's how it's done.
That men keep fighting, yet go on living . . .

2.

In the car—the nation's jabbering first-class folk:
Biedermeier dames with high-brow specs,
A trouser stripe under a general's black cloak,
A Polish moustache grown for honor and respect.
And every eye stares out like a lorgnette.
Forever static, set in place to stay,
Each body a shell, a sculptor's maquette.
But the man inside's long moved away.
Onto the trains the bourgeois clamber
In silence, battering down Russia's door,
And with his pipe in hand he stands there—
A vagabond, a Pipeman, and a *voyageur* . . .

3.

Fall. Bare. A young calf sipping water,
And forest-blue tints the distant spaces.
The dead train drags itself toward the border
And dies away at every station.
A ruined little depot. Hushed. Late.
The rain wets both telegraph wires and gutters,
A shadow flickers by on houses' shutters,
And gliding past, a bayonet's metallic blade.
A Bolshevik! His squinty eyes look wary,
A cigarette between his teeth.
And in the car it's Pipeman who sits solitary,
The only one not shaking in his seat.

4.

Absorbed in novels and poetic diction
For nineteen years, was our noble Pipeman,
Until the world, too, seemed like fiction
With civil wars for men to fight in.
On whispers of watchwords and flags he meditates,
While wandering his hometown aimless,
On conversations led by .38s—
He tailed all like Pinkerton the shamus.
Old worn-out cannons clatter down the avenues
While in a ditch a German helmet wallows to and fro.
Our Pipeman feels at ease and quite amused.
He's Rinaldo Rinaldini set to go.

5.

Suddenly he's in a railcar. He's off to study,
Off to Europe. Each must do his thing: a skylark croons,
A Bolshevik makes revolutions, and Pipeman—it's in his blood—
Must study. The day goes by. Metallic hues.
Now all is swallowed up by his hungry eye:
A trestle. In a valley, a White Russian fir.
And over there a murky creek suddenly flies by.
In haste the telegraph poles speed backward.
Home ends here! If anything dissatisfies, then
Keep quiet, pal, quiet like this traveling clan,
As quiet as in the distance, by the white horizon,
Three silvered pines, branchless and alone . . .

II.

BERLIN

6.

Vivat Europa! O'er the ocean swam
Merchants from Moscow to the Kurfürstendamm;
Millionaires and check-books and wine by the barrel—
And from Lohojsk, Childe Harold.
Like all of those who have here flown,
For every moment give ye praise!
Now Pipeman stands at Bahnhof Zoo
And stares Europe in the face.
O Wond'rous Land! Where electricity passes
Through wires, and through arteries—champagne—
Where Marx and Engels cheer the working masses
And shop-keeps swear by Kant's immortal name.

7.

A summer evening. A thrust of hands
At Bahnhof Zoo. Here, wafting from the lower spheres,
The piercing S-Bahn, and the trams,
With hats, more hats, and freshly-shaven beards.
Traffic barking as electric ads confuse
And write themselves into the skies.
In the heat of Berlin *Tammuz*,
"Alles Jut!" "Prospérité!" "All Right!" a radio cries.
It's nine: His Nuremberg watch marks this—
The fires start to blaze in cabarets.
The first full drunken dawn-to-darkness.
Spent Pipeman learning Berlin ways.

8.

Childe Harolds by nature eat quite seldom,
And so does this Childe Harold of Dysna;
Lean, lanky, and dark to those who beheld him,
He's clean, although his shave's abysmal,
There wafts from him a tailor's scent
Bequeathed by legacies of toil and want—
Now Pipeman's found a Bellevue room to rent
And washes dishes in a restaurant.
In the sultry blue of a Berlin evening
He's now grown continental, well, nearly;
To be a European, all he's lacking:
Pyjamas, a dog, and a dose of V.D.

9.

Bellevue is quiet. High balconies and curtains,
A privy-counselor rambles here;
And much like spiders, rentiers lurk in
Their leather webs *à la Empire*.
There in his car a chauffeur snoozes,
A dowager throws crumbs into the Spree;
Here you quietly drink your Patzenhofer brew
As you while away the day.
By the water, in a bright disposition,
You'll find Pipeman. He's immersed
In his book and feels fine—in opposition
To himself, his book, the universe.

10.

Pipeman's hostess went gray long ago.
An old young-lady, she never married.
Miss Weichert sits in her room done Rococo
As she smokes and feeds her canary.
Miss Weichert's twenty years short of a century,
Canary must be nearing forty.
The two sit candidly deploring:
No future generations, so much to regret.
One spring—Silesia . . . Water . . . Pastures . . .
A second-lieutenant . . . Once was, but gone away . . .
Now little birdie's white and so cocksure.
It's as though Miss Weichert were forever gray.

11.

He's twenty-six, she's eighty—all the same.
This hostess loves her *Russe* with zeal,
Each day she brings his morning meal,
While canary hangs his head in shame.
As he's eating, she's intent and sees
His hot and fervent lips sip and smack—
And she can picture the Siberian freeze,
With samovars and bears and Cossacks . . .
Then his mistress shuffles out in haste
And on her gilt Rococo sleep alights,
And only the old canary pipes
While Pipeman goes off to wash more plates.

12.

The dark, handsome Russian's in a rush.
Barely tying his cravat,
He takes a seat atop an omnibus
And leafs through the *Berliner Tageblatt*.
You speed right through the *Brandenburger Tor*
And under its victorious horses running mad
(*O Gloria!* It is terribly clear
That all great victors die, both good and bad . . .)
He hears how in the sunshine of Savigny-Platz
Berliner birds are gladly singing;
He sits there still with *Götz von Berlichingen*,
Rejoicing, purring like contented cats.

13.

He's got some friends. Two worn knights-errant
Of the arts. Two starving folks:
Jussuf Abbo and Erich Dern—
The watch-cogs of a time that stopped and broke.
Abbo is an Arab visionary
A tender sculptor with two moonlit hands,
A shorter guy with curly hair;
He strives in clay toward Eastern lands.
And Dern just cannot keep his chin up;
A quiet German, hardly says a word;
A cultivated man of Europe,
With quicksilver in his spinal cord.

14.

They spend the evenings in a café
Where faces swim in gentle smoke.
Where ideas, too, can swim backstroke—
They sit and talk of old Lao-Tze.
The words glide by sharp and lean,
They let fly choice aphorisms;
As all draw forth their witticisms
From an ancient thought-machine.
Berliner poets polish to a glow
The finest of their word-hewn shavings.—
But dozing at the table Abbo
And Dern are as quiet as a grave.

15.

At night in the clubs illuminated,
The jazz bands circle Pipeman, thronging.
Berliner nights in *cafés-chantants* and—
Pal, isn't this sophisticated?
Here sit the masters of the marketplaces;
From their broad necks depend their coats,
Their pointed skulls suspend their faces,
And richly wrinkled chins and throats.
Each one is a credenza stacked with meat
With rippling booze-sonata harmonies,
With jazz outcries from the colonies
In the darkling fires of Negro dancing beats.

16.

Below white tucked-in napkins, plates reflect
The brilliant shine of skin off the bald-pated.
There, in emerald chills a bottle of *Sekt*—
Pal, isn't this sophisticated?
O, what a riot! What a song!
The cherry brandy bleeds into the crystal:
Lehn deine Wang' an meine Wang,
You, Gretchen, with your nose so little,
My mind's distilled by the band,
The shimmy's why we were created!
And Pipeman lingers in the Bar Am Strand—
Pal, isn't this sophisticated?

17.

Untiringly had Shmulik Pipeman striven,
For nothing, nothing, nothing.
Abbo has just his hands absorbed in thinking.
But Dern teaches him the craft of living:
Don't mix or mingle and accept another's kindness;
Friend, buy yourself a German shepherd dog
Who'll guide you as you walk behind;
And don't read books—your mind will fog!
For doing what's been done before us
Works just while playing Préférence;
O, be a gentleman par excellence
And when everyone laughs, don't join the chorus.

18.

The teacher loves the trappings of high thinking,
An aphorism, a play on words;
In the theater of a culture that's sinking
Dern's spent his time beneath the boards.
Instructs the Arab in new ideas,
And enlightens Pipeman, too,
In smoke that's philosophic-blue.
Of listen-now-*ego-sum-vias*.
All over awe-inspiring grand:
Spengler, Keyserling, and Lasker-Schüler—
The phrases that can leap like rams,
But make the tired blood run chiller.

19.

Now Pipeman hears the crazy times:
Berlin convulses in fits of screams;
Der deutsche Michel screams atop the chimes;
Below him scream the theaters and museums.
Granach frets on stage in a wild demeanor
While in a mad-scene Moissi sings,
Like a sickly pallid ballerina,
And long-dead poetry always stinks . . .
It's the demise of distant roars.
But here it dies a death that's sweet—
Expressionism strides with its red feet,
Dada with its pulled-down drawers.

20.

Here's a museum in a chilled retreat—
The Kaiser Friedrich: doorway rarely crossed,
Where every Sunday Pipeman meets
A tall lady who's cold as frost.
Throughout antique graces gleam glorious,
Antique graces glorious gleam out through,
The lady sighs for Florentines before us,
The lady cries at Botticelli's blue.
And Pipeman is gracious as well—
About the spaces he paces, fortified,
A bit he knew, a lick he felt,
As for the rest—he whistled by.

21.

Till now did young Childe Harold thirst:
To try his luck and to indulge some,
To take a bite of each side of the earth,
And to revel in the taste of every crumb.
And there fermented the obscure brew
Of Senderl with Lomonosov;
Electric Europe's fresh and new
To a Narovlya Philosophe.
Just once at night by a late bright moon,
He said to himself and to his sheets:
—I feel just like an air-balloon,
Whose string is loosened, and set free.

III.

KRIUCHKOV

22.

It was at the corner, where the gas-lamp's heat
Burned the last few hours of semi-darkness,
Where Abbo led him first to meet
A blonde, young bird from Tauenzienstraße.
All wrapped up in a white fichu
And narrow-tipped Vienna shoes,
Her laughter she just couldn't throttle,
Or her babble polyglottal.
And he just looked at her askew,
Without a shred of comprehension
When she whispered soft to Pipeman:
Je voo zem and *I loff yoo!*

23.

Then at Abbo's studio, a soiree;
On oriental rugs imported,
Childe Harold of Smorgon himself disported.
In the bright blue break of day
The last frayed nerves frayed even thinner
Losing luster in the cold dawn's shine,
Like all the strewn and finished tins or
Like these bottles tapped of wine.
And the blonde, young bird, half drifting off
Mumbled from her green, soft cushion:
—*Sag, lieber Bub, ich möchte's wissen,*
Aren't you the Cossack, Herr Kriuchkov?

24.

"*Ich bin nicht, Liebchen, Herr Kriuchkov,*
Now sleep tight, my love, and have no fear . . .
I'm just a Cossack who's come from Shklov;
Mein Papa war ein alter Kavalier
Von Iron-Shears, known for slinging
Taters out of white-hot flames,
And, as is the Order of Needles' fame,
He accompanied life with song and singing . . .
—*Und, Liebchen, weiß*: those sweet, sad tones,
Endured for however long, I cannot tell.
We flew from his marble castle one by one,
Each of us, to the fires of hell."

IV.

WEDDING

25.

The sky's still black and cold and wide—
But bike wheels start to scrape backstreets and
Gloomy laborers spill out and ride
Into dismal factories. And
On every corner—the dim gaslight,
A green *Schupo*, and a hooker;
In any city where you look, you're
Going to find these three at the end of the night . . .
Half that night—in cabarets
With jazz bands and with French letters,
Half with Borsig's dark steam trains
And in the AEG plant's fetters.

26.

And on the gray blocks of Wedding and Neukölln,
An enormous sun begins to shine
Like Prince von Hohenzollern Wilhelm,
Reviewing *soldaten*, dressed to the nines.
A postman. A keg of beer.
With his heavy pipe beside the door
The stubby barman sleeps while standing—
Half an angel, half a hangman.
Maggots, like black poppy seeds,
Thrive in the liverwurst and butter;
Up in a room a guitar plays off-key
A wet blanket drips into the gutter.

27.

—Now, August Thyssen has police,
Also Reichswehr, this Thyssen!
You a member of the KPD?
Tell me, Grete, and I'll listen.
You love the Luna Park with all your suitors,
To visit Circus Busch and have a ball;
Comrade Remmele speaks well,
Comrade Neumann speaks even better.
But you still love me—But, now hear why:
We share one pillow that we rest on
I'd like one thing only, if unemployed,—
I'll tell you, Grete, will you listen?

28.

A cactus, limp like a broken fist.
The wind tangles with a modest curtain.
Between is a child—yet no child—who sits,
With spindly bones and sallow skin.
Is this a child or melting matter,
With hollow eyes like specks of dust?
Already molten lead is being set for
A bullet that will pierce his future guts.
In this land a nation's force waits in its cast,
That will burst out when it's ripened.
Like a snow-white seagull in a whirlwind
Charges out and shrieks and laughs.

29.

Meanwhile all is still. The rage asleep
Coiled up like a boa behind a glass,
Like a sprawling cactus mass,
Yet when it rouses, it's set to leap . . .
And in the pubs a sleeve wipes clean
The beer foam off a moustache. From pipes and
Cigarettes the smoke solidifies and
Misery keeps its head bowed deep.
A slogan's heard every now and then.
Some puffs on a pipe, calm but rigid;
And on one pipe, faithfully depicted:
Herr Feldmarschall von Mackensen.

30.

Amidst the pipes and tobacco smoke
Someone rolls a light and gropes for matches.
Wearing weathered work boots stands a pale bloke
And adjusts his rounded Radek glasses.
Then he's on a table. The pub ignites.
The Party. An order. A demonstration.
—One lone worker is a job and deprivation,
But a thousand can be dynamite!
The years are beaten and in barrels contained,
The barrel-chested bossman stands aghast—
The bar empties out. The rage remains,
Like a boa curled up behind a glass.

31.

And Wedding, with a fist under its pillow,
Goes to bed. It's already late at night
And a giant sword hangs over Europe.
The gates and the pubs are all shut tight—
And Germany is peaceful. The State pays heed.
Who's changing guard at the Moabit Prison?
Stinnes, Krupp, and Thyssen . . .
In sleep—the echo of heavy marching feet.
The German moon hovers in the sky.
A brutal light. A dour profile.
And narrow alleys get some shut-eye.
Is this a dream, or gray, real life?

V.

HE'S IN LOVE

32.

He's in love. In the Tiergarten in a quiet spot
With sighs of love he meditated:
What is the source of my rose-colored thoughts?
And my divine sorrow—what is its basis?
Yet, like that old lion in his pen dozing off,
Or like those kindly bears in folktales,
I secretly give the finger as I scoff
At my dim dreams and holy grails,
As always. Still I am dedicated
To the proud, great tailor masses . . .
You, O blonde bird of Tauenzienstraße!
You, O dainty, china maiden!

33.

The gloomy pelican, homesick in its pen,
Hides his sorrow with his flat, long bill.
So, too, the Berliner Pipeman
In his longing is fashionable . . .
He gazes with dark and tender eyes,
In his hand the pipe still smolders
Beside a jasmine's beauty, the beholder
Aches gallantly like Conrad Veidt.
On this clear, blue June day's walk,
He's now grown continental, well almost;
To be a European, all he lacks is—
A wrinkled, stout English bulldog.

34.

It's lunchtime and nearly dead from hunger
Childe Harold can think of nothing else
But to sip a snifter of liqueur,
Bathing others in his brightness.
Commotion. Noise. A green *Schupo*.
Trolley-cars. Signs. Flashing lights.
To Aschinger's for some split-pea soup. O,
Aschinger's! Off the tram to you he alights.
Childe Harold of Dysna enters in,
And—to hell with longing and homesickness,
When one looks into your dishes
And tastes your green split peas in person!

35.

Here, with their threadbare, tattered shirts,
A young herd grazes on *Löffelerbsen*;
Accountants after a full day's work
Dream of a warm room to piss in.
A small-time broker. A student with a book.
A quiet war-widow sits over yonder
With praying hands and a pious look,
Like Raphael's Sistine Madonna.
There's a staring, starving painter
Watching people eat. There a hooker sleeps.
Those who have the cash all feed here
Amid this European trash heap.

36.

Afterwards, Pipeman felt indisposed
In a suffocating spot that chokes him.
Palely shivered on the sofa,
Surrounded by books and newspapers.
He read Stirner, he read Heine,
Read Külpe and *Jerusalem*.
Suddenly he hears: *Je voo zem!*
And Childe Harold feels like crying.
Then a knock. Fräulein Weichert declares:
It's *Goethe Tag* today, a Goethe celebration.
She asks her *Russe* if he would care
To devote fifteen minutes to declamation?

37.

Today is Goethe Day. Delicately
Crisp moments fall from the Rococo clock face.
Fräulein Weichert reads *Roman Elegies*
As she sits beside the fireplace.
The Poet's *Geist* rests in the curtains,
And in every spotless, polished glass.
Even the shadowy walls hear the words of
This man of letters unsurpassed.
Only old canary seems to have forgotten
To sing what must be sung loud and true.
As *Geheimrat* Goethe sings, I'll sing too
Of all his years of Faustian drama.

38.

Under his breath Herr Pipeman then said:
A pox on the Jews and upon the French,
For your great king has been hounded
And *deutscher Michel* frolics in his pants . . .
But I foresee a new age yet stirs,
When every hankie will be adorned
With a Goethe quote. O, tender escort
Of two million German boots and spurs—
For Togoland will kneel before his highness,
And in the nightclub singer's ear will be heard a
Weary cub from a league of lions
Reciting verses from Great Goethe!

39.

We kneel before thee. O, *Absolute Geist!*
Before thy servants in this city—
Game birds with love letters clasped
In their emerald bills, the lapidaries
Of words. Soulful. Happy songsters
And keeners who so sweetly made
The suppers of emperors
And princesses, and laid them at their feet
As stealthily as old billy goats
In virtuous exaltation . . .
You, O birds of all the nations!
You finches in black tail coats!

40.

Yet the great *Geist*—to me it's clear—
Drags itself deeper and deeper down;
It's a concave mirror, in which appear
The silent forces from underground.
It's a promise. It's a call.
It's the greeting of paths wiped away.
It's the echo of a brawl.
It's the great body's reverie.
In gray libraries it intoxicates you
And darkly chatters like an old crow . . .
There are nearly a hundred works that can wake you
(But in Yiddish there's not one to show).

41.

By now I know, how a thousand times it's
Possible to dig about for life's solution,
Like chickens digging in detritus . . .
And never coming to resolution.
Put their feet forward in the darkness
The "heads in hieroglyphic caps" of Heine,
Harnessing storms and lightning flashes,
Outside them, sublimity, divinity, and the divine.
Out from its spider-woven webbing
Radiates, like a holy flame at night,
Your outlook, your will for living,
And professorial insight.

42.

Mademoiselle, O, I am ill,
Ill, like this young century and indisposed.
To myself I even once proposed
A leap from my dad's window-sill.
Recklessness, daring, and youthful folly,
A bit of Blok, some Schopenhauer,
Peretz, Spinoza, and kabbala.
Rootless, despair and more despair.
Something waits to be comprehended—
But soon all will brightly shine out.
When my youth has been expended,
And I'm left with nothing but doubt.

43.

"Dixi!" he said, then meekly smiled. Our Pipeman
Wiped the cold sweat off his forehead:
—Perhaps some valerian! . . .
And hot tears began to shed,
Dripping like a willow by the water . . .
He fought them back. He denied them.
He sat pale by the hearthstone,
And overwhelmed, Childe Harold cried some.
Miss Weichert stared through her lorgnette,
And mean canary took to warble.
O, Heavens! Even a Jack from an old card-deck
Began to sing then of his squalor.

44.

At midnight the room was sleeping soundly,
A moonface dreamed upon the walls
Confused, off-kilter, and confounded
Our Pipeman raced down stairs and halls.
And dopily with his two chums
Spent the night with criminal masters,
Drank in the squares with maids and bums
And knocked them back until well-plastered.
Dern, in his inebriation,
Parsed Hegesias of Cyrene
Till they were led to the police station
After having made a scene.

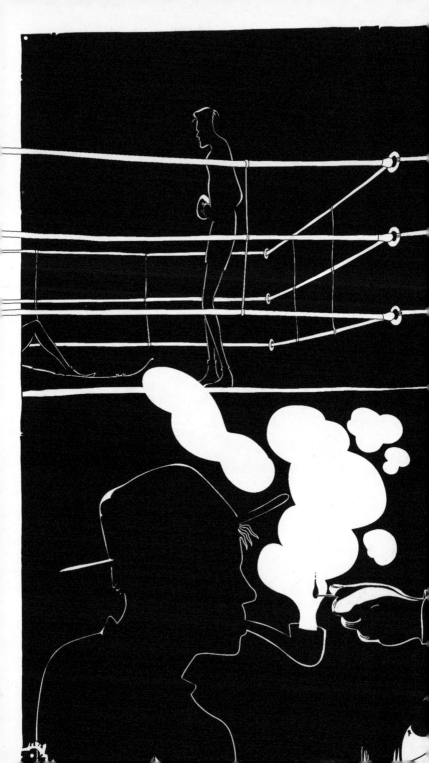

VI.

PANEM ET CIRCENSES

45.

Vivat, Europa! Panem et
Circenses. A joke for all great jokers.
Lonely the worker lies in bed,
Put to sleep by his Patzenhofer.
The grim courtyard echoes the factory's din,
A blue axe chops wood for an arena.
Here boxers will pummel and win
While the masses belch butter with sardines and
How radiant! Persian rugs beneath the chairs.
They've cleaned the alleys before the entrance.
The lanterns flicker. The masses flare
Their nostrils, sensing their opponents.

46.

And then: With leathered fists in the ring
They gore each other just like oxen;
Nimbly one lets a left hook swing
The crowd adores the algebra of boxing . . .
KNOCKOUT! A splendid blow to his thick skull.
Let us praise good taste and culture:
In Rembrandt hues, somber and dull,
Ripple waves of musculature.
O! The punch explodes into his spine,
Ringing deeply into his core.
In the dull lanterns' light he lies supine.
As the masses beg for more.

47.

KNOCKOUT! A heap of heads listen
All around the boxing ring,
The boxer jabs, letting punches sing,
He pounds the flesh keys, a musician.
In a flash—*THUNK!* A boxer decked.
Collapse. A gasp. In the courtyard
The crowd dies out. Someone checks
For a pulse on the splayed-out forearm.
The lanterns flicker and sputter gas-less
They putter off lonely with a hiss———
Childe Harold had screamed with the masses
And he became a Sss . . . socialist.

THE OTHER GERMANY

48.

A hatred lives here—a sliver of cut glass,
It shines like a ruby with blood and in panic . . .
Night descends and the steel moon casts
A gossamer silvery strand on
The church spires and the prison latches.
A hatred lives here without end, without walls.
Without escape . . . A shiv flashes—
A bloodied knife pulled in a brawl
Then vanishes . . . A shot. Placards on doorways.
In the darkness—a red flag.
Workers in groups. Half a gate lies
Broken under a crumbling balcony's sag.

49.

The narrow alleys are silenced.
No rustling, no shuffling, no uproar.
The yawn of night school is all that's noticed,
And a projector beam at the door.
A steely eye. With its beam, bright yet muted,
The night divides into a rift,
Where latest posters get glued up,
Where workers are changing shift,
And between the beams that stripe out
Across and beyond these local ports,
A laborer sits with his pipe lit
On an overturned trolley car.

50.

A battle. The *Schupo* is stationed
On Nettelbeckstraße. Glaring vans.
In darkness—an aggregation
Of rifles, directives, and hands.
A lieutenant with field glasses
Leads the dead on a Citroën,
"Clear the streets!" The night spasms.
—Partner! Nothing's doin'.
These lousy shits just aren't dying . . .
—Partner! I heard something, did you?
Just then: A flowerpot comes flying
And cracks a porcine skull in two.

51.

And then: ranks pour out into the night
A shadow shadows another shadow,
A knot of shapes in the darkness. A salvo.
And there: entangled in a wire,
The concretion of a car. A holler
Penetrates the night, a stampede of feet.
The same blood-crusted fringes cover
All the battered heads that bleed—
Screaming: "*Grüne!*" . . . Then not a murmur
Heard after. Ursa Major in the sky,
Field glasses, a revolver—down nearby.
A trace of blood . . . and nothing further.

52.

Day breaks. With his head on a scrawny knee,
Schulze lies unseen in the courtyards, crumpled—
A bullet careened through his temples,
A product of a similar industry.
Day breaks. Heinze stands at the kiosk:
—On that barricade I'd gladly croak
For just one goddamned German smoke.
He sulks and tugs at the padlock.
Day breaks. A kneeling drunken maid
Beside the tree-lined street:
—Her father—on the barricade,
And a brother—imprisoned in Moabit.

53.

Day breaks. Wedding's sun rises in distress.
Wedding bleeds with the daylight's waking,
Dripping blood like a maimed beast
At the forest edge. Dreams dissipating
Like water. Young men stand to lift a
Bloodied paw to a mouth:
—What we have now—is foul,
And what we've had—is fiction!
Day breaks, and through pink dust
Drab, cold colors stream: a streak of orange
Where a door was ripped from a door hinge,
And blue where a lintel's dressed in rust.

54.

And later on, the sunlight washed off
The funereal face of distress;
The young men, their hands in their pockets,
With fags between their lips,
Laughed loudly outside in the squares, and
At the workers' committee:
—*Wir wollen dem Dreck auskehren*
From every single German city . . .
And neckties and booklets and banners
Fluttered red and far;
And songs in the courtyards were chanted
In the key of the coming class war.

55.

Now daytime . . . A dreadful tune is lifted
From cellars, on garrets, and rooftops.
Just a gesture. Just a motion. Just steps as
A million spilled out of their hideouts.
Just breath. Just loathing. Icy gazes.
Quivering in red. Flags upon flags
Through alleys and squares. A mass of faces,
A frigid, ash-gray million zags.
A door barged down. In Wedding
The courtyards emptied. A mass,
A million stand, a whirlwind eddies
Round the fingers of an open fist.

56.

Who stands watch at Moabit Prison?
Night and day we hear the heavy feet
Of Stinnes, Krupp, and Thyssen . . .
And of all your guards, Moabit, Moabit . . .
France has steel that's stainless,
Belgium coke and Germany lead.
So often the worker wracked by pain is
Led to the abattoir, left for dead.
The old prisons have devoured us,
Just like you, O Fatherland Great,
Neukölln sings its hate. And the hour has
Come: for Wedding the hangman awaits.

57.

Wrath lies heavy inside a hairy belly,
And suddenly—a silence unto death.
In the gleam of an upraised axe
The city noise is suppressed.
Such gruesome beauty: A stand of trees
When a storm tore in deeper
And on the trunks is etched the shuttering cold
A phosphorescent cipher.
A flash, another flash . . . Every movement is
As petrified as Laocoön.
The frozen leap of a beast,
The cold, ash-gray million.

58.

Upon Alexanderplatz she shines,
Staring wisely down on the masses—
The little bird of Tauenzienstraße
With all her friends so sweet and kind.
And there's Dern, the sage of the café,
Powdered pallid like a ballerina.
Abbo and Pipeman in their *vestons Bébé*
Wearing neckties of what else but green.
Over Dern bows the little sparrow,
Her slender body pretty and tall,
Her little mouth, blood-red and small,
Her eyes—bright little arrows.

59.

"C'est charmant!" The demonstration
Winds over miles of Berliner streets;
In fragments lies half the nation,
And the other half lifts its feet:
In caps, in brown, work clothes and smocks,
Unshaven and rash,
No churches, no prisons, no padlocks,
No rent, no checks, no cash.
Here marches the metal worker of Emil Henning,
And here marches a stoker of the A.E.G.
Neither has a single pfenning,
Or wears a *veston Bébé*.

60.

No velvet, no silken pants,
Just corduroy and Manchester cloth,
And then every orchestra bursts forth
With its hot, bloodletting brass.
Cymbals—simply screeching hatred
The drum like a bear in its cage,
And flowing out clear and plain is
The sluggish loathing of bass.
And suddenly—a silence unto dread,
A salvo. A command. Men lie upon asphalt.
And a stream of blood pours from a head.
Death. A million quiet as a vault.

61.

At night. Four thin shadows rise
And at a Wedding pub they meet.
Wearing cufflinks and neckties,
Sitting on an old oaken seat.
And Childe Harold says: Comrades.
Man is eternally good,
Man's blood has been spilled, friends,
And man will spill more blood.
So drink up, mates, let's keep drinking;
And quietly he said:
Man already starts stinking
Long before he's even dead.

62.

At night. On city squares and corners, there's
A demonstration in groups of four:
O, Europa, Europa for you we bear
Your javelin, your mighty sword.
On beds unmade and rumpled,
How you sin—you old Sodom!
Down with Beethoven and with Goethe!
Down with the cathedral in Cologne!
The distant skies are turning gray
And we turn gray along with them;
We—the last of wolves that bay
In the ruins of the system.

NOTES

Title.
> *Dysna*:
> City in the north of modern-day Belarus.

Stanza 4.
> *Rinaldo Rinaldini*:
> Swashbuckling brigand in the novel *Rinaldo Rinaldini, der Räuber-Hauptmann* (1797)—*Rinaldo Rinaldini, the Robber Captain*—by novelist Christian August Vulpius (1762–1827).

Stanza 6.
> *Kurfürstendamm*:
> Boulevard in Berlin, one of the primary commercial arteries of the city.

> *Lohojsk*:
> Town in the center of modern-day Belarus.

> *Bahnhof Zoo*:
> Railway station in Berlin, adjacent to the zoo.

Stanza 7.
> *S-Bahn*:
> Railway system within the city of Berlin.

> *Tammuz*:
> Hebrew month corresponding to the summer period from mid-June to mid-July.

Stanza 8.
> *Bellevue*:
> Area around the Bellevue Palace in central Berlin.

Stanza 9.

Spree:
River running through Berlin.

Patzenhofer:
Brewery, formerly located in central Berlin.

Stanza 12.

Berliner Tageblatt:
Influential liberal German newspaper.

Brandenburger Tor:
Brandenburg Gate; famous monument in west-central Berlin erected in the late eighteenth century.

Savigny-Platz:
Square in a residential area of Berlin in the district of Charlottenburg.

Götz von Berlichingen:
Nickname of Gottfried von Berlichingen (1480–1562) whose military exploits are recounted in an autobiography, which was subsequently dramatized in the eponymous play (1773) by Johann Wolfgang von Goethe.

Stanza 13.

Jussuf Abbo:
Jewish avant-garde artist and sculptor who moved from his native Palestine to Germany in 1911 and worked there before he fled in 1935.

Stanza 16.

Lehn deine Wang' an meine Wang':
"Lean your cheek 'pon my cheek"; first line of a love lyric by Heinrich Heine.

Stanza 18.

Spengler:
Oswald Spengler (1880–1936); influential historian and
philosopher.

Keyserling:
Eduard von Keyserling (1855–1918); German writer and
proto-Impressionist.

Lasker-Schüler:
Else Lasker-Schüler (1869–1945); one of the foremost
German Expressionist poets.

Stanza 19.

Der deutsche Michel:
"German Michel"; national personification of the German
people, as Marianne is to the French or John Bull to the
English.

Granach:
Alexander Granach (1890–1945); German stage and film
actor of the interwar period.

Moissi:
Alexander Moissi (1879–1935); famous stage actor, prominent
in Max Rheinhardt's Deutsches Theater in Berlin.

Stanza 20.

Kaiser-Friedrich:
Kaiser-Friedrich-Museum, known today as the Bode Museum,
is an historical fine-art museum on the Museum Island in
central Berlin.

Stanza 21.

Senderl:
Character in Mendele Moykher-Sforim's novel *Travels of
Benjamin III*, a Yiddish send-up of *Don Quixote* in which
Senderl plays the quick-witted Sancho Panza figure.

Lomonosov:
Mikhail Lomonosov (1711–1765); multitalented Russian scientist and writer.

Narovlya:
Small town in the southeast of modern-day Belarus.

Section III.
Kriuchkov:
Kuzma Kriuchkov (1890–1919); a Don Cossack who for his heroism fighting the Germans in the First World War was awarded the Russian Cross of Saint George.

Stanza 22.
Tauenzienstraße:
A large avenue in central Berlin at the end of Kurfürstendamm, south of the zoo, and popular in the interwar period with artists and intellectuals.

Stanza 23.
Smorgon:
City in the northwest of modern-day Belarus, where Kulbak was born.

Sag', lieber Bub, ich möchte's wissen:
"Tell me, dear boy, I'd like to know"

Stanza 24.
Ich bin nicht, Liebchen, Herr Kriuchkov:
"Darling, I'm not Herr Kriuchkov"

Mein Papa war ein alter Kavalier / von Iron-Shears:
"My father was an old squire of Iron-Shears"

Und, Liebchen, weiß:
"And, darling, just know . . ."

Section IV.
Wedding:
Working-class district in west central Berlin known in the
interwar period for its militancy and Communist sympathy.

Stanza 25.
Schupo:
Abbreviation for *Schutzpolizei*, "Security Police."

French letters:
A "French letter" is a euphemism for a condom.

Borsig:
August Borsig (1804–1854); German industrialist, producer
of steam locomotives.

AEG:
Allgemeine Elektricitäts-Gesellschaft; founded in Berlin
in 1883, major producer of German electrical equipment
and transmission systems.

Stanza 26.
Neukölln:
Southeastern borough of Berlin.

Stanza 27.
August Thyssen:
August Thyssen (1842–1926); German industrialist, producer
of iron and steel.

KPD:
Abbreviation for the *Kommunistische Partei Deutschlands*: the
Communist Party of Germany.

Luna Park:
Luna Park was an amusement park operating in Berlin
between 1909 and 1933, reputed to have been among
Europe's largest.

Comrade Remmele:
Hermann Remmele (1880–1939); German politician and
member of the KPD.

Comrade Neumann:
Heinz Neumann (1902–1937); German journalist and
politician, member of the KPD.

Stanza 29.
Feldmarschall von Mackensen:
August von Mackensen (1849–1945); German Field Marshall,
a prominent figure in the First World War.

Stanza 30.
Radek glasses:
Karl Radek (1885–1939); a Marxist and Communist activist
in Germany and Russia, visually associated with his round,
horn-rimmed glasses.

Stanza 31.
Moabit Prison:
Moabit is a neighborhood in central Berlin closely associated
with the prison for the criminal court located there.

Stinnes:
Hugo Stinnes (1870–1924); German industrialist, involved
in fuels for energy production.

Krupp:
The Krupp family's eponymous company, involved in many
areas of industrial production from steel to armaments, was
one of Europe's largest in the interwar period.

Stanza 32.
Tiergarten:
A large urban park in Berlin which includes the zoo
(in German, *Tiergarten*).

Stanza 33.
   Conrad Veidt:
   Conrad Veidt (1893–1943); famous German film actor.

Stanza 34.
   Aschinger's:
   Large restaurant business opened by the brothers Aschinger—
   Carl and August—in Berlin in 1892.

Stanza 35.
   Löffelerbsen:
   Thick yellow-pea soup from Berlin.

Stanza 36.
   Stirner:
   Max Stirner (1806–1856); German philosopher, best known
   for his book *The Ego and Its Own*.

   Heine:
   Heinrich Heine (1797–1856); one of the most famous
   German Romantic poets.

   Külpe:
   Oswald Külpe (1862–1915); noted experimental psychologist.

   Jerusalem:
   Jerusalem (1783) is a work of political philosophy by Jewish
   philosopher Moses Mendelssohn (1729–1786) concerning
   the relation of the individual to the enlightened state.

   Goethe:
   Johann Wolfgang von Goethe (1749–1832); arguably the
   German language's most famous poet.

Stanza 37.
   Geist:
   "Spirit" in both a concrete and figurative sense.

Geheimrat:
"Privy Councilor"; Goethe served on the Privy Council of
Karl August, Duke of Saxe-Weimar.

Stanza 38.
Togoland:
German colony in coastal West Africa from 1884–1914.

Stanza 41.
heads in hieroglyphic caps:
a reference to a line from Heine's poem *Die Nordsee*, satirizing
philosophers.

Stanza 42.
Blok:
Alexander Blok (1880–1921); Russian lyric poet.

Schopenhauer:
Arthur Schopenhauer (1788–1860); influential post-Kantian
philosopher.

Peretz:
Yitskhok Leybush Peretz (1852–1915); neo-Romantic writer
and cultural figure; one of the three canonical "Classic"
Yiddish writers.

Spinoza:
Baruch Spinoza (1632–1677); Jewish Rationalist philosopher.

Stanza 44.
Hegesias of Cyrene:
Hegesias of Cyrene (c. 3rd century BCE); Greek philosopher,
reputed to have written a book on the preferability of death
to life, a book which was so persuasive that it induced many
people to take their own lives.

Stanza 54.
> *Wir wollen dem Dreck auskehren*:
> "We want to sweep away the filth"

Stanza 58.
> *Alexanderplatz*:
> Large square in central Berlin, known in the interwar period for its nightlife.

Stanza 62.
> *Cathedral in Cologne*:
> The Cologne Cathedral is one of the largest Gothic cathedrals in Europe and a noted German symbol.

BIOGRAPHIES

Moyshe Kulbak (1896–1937), one of the great poets of the modern explosion of Yiddish creativity in the early twentieth century, was born in Smorgon, in the Vilna Province of the Russian Empire (today in Belarus). The author of six volumes of poetry he was also a successful playwright, novelist, and translator. Committed to the ideals of revolution, he left Poland for the Soviet Union in 1927. He settled in Minsk where he lived for the next decade until his arrest in September 1937 on charges of disloyalty to the state and espionage. He was executed the following month.

Robert Adler Peckerar is the director of the cultural education organization, Yiddishkayt, headquartered in Los Angeles. He holds a PhD in comparative literature from the University of California at Berkeley and is the creator of the Wallis Annenberg Helix Fellowship, an annual interdisciplinary mobile arts residency based out of Minsk, Belarus.

Boris Dralyuk is a literary translator and the Executive Editor of *Los Angeles Review of Books*. He is the editor of *1917: Stories and Poems from the Russian Revolution*, co-editor of *The Penguin Book of Russian Poetry*, and translator of volumes by Isaac Babel, Mikhail Zoshchenko, and other authors.

Beynish is an artist living at the same time as you.